Incredible Arachnids

John Townsend

Raintree

www.raintreepublishers.co.uk
Visit our website to find out more information about Raintree books.

To order:
☎ Phone 44 (0) 1865 888113
▤ Send a fax to 44 (0) 1865 314091
▣ Visit the Raintree Bookshop at **www.raintreepublishers.co.uk** to browse our
catalogue and order online.

First published in Great Britain by Raintree Publishers,
Halley Court, Jordan Hill, Oxford, OX2 8EJ,
part of Harcourt Education Ltd.
Raintree is a registered trademark of Harcourt
Education Ltd.

© Harcourt Education Ltd 2005
The moral right of the proprietor has been asserted.

Produced for Raintree Publishers by Discovery Books Ltd
Editorial: Louise Galpine, Elisabeth Taylor,
Charlotte Guillain, and Diyan Leake
Expert reader: Michael Chinery
Design: Victoria Bevan, Keith Williams (sprout.uk.com
Limited), and Michelle Lisseter
Picture Research: Maria Joannou and Kay Altwegg
Production: Duncan Gilbert and Jonathan Smith
Printed and bound in China by South China
Printing Company
Originated by Repro Multi Warna

ISBN 1 844 43451 6 (hardback)
09 08 07 06 05
10 9 8 7 6 5 4 3 2 1

ISBN 1 844 43471 0 (paperback)
09 08 07 06 05
10 9 8 7 6 5 4 3 2 1

British Library Cataloguing in Publication Data
Townsend, John
Incredible arachnids. – (Freestyle express. Incredible
creatures)
595.4
A full catalogue record for this book is available from the
British Library.

This levelled text is a version of Freestyle:
Incredible creatures series: Incredible arachnids.

Photo acknowledgements
The publisher would like to thank the following for
permission to reproduce photographs: Ant Photolibrary
p. 35 top; California Academy of Science p. 32 (John S.
Reid); Corbis pp. 16 (David A. Northcott), 16–17 (Galen
Rowell); FLPA pp. 11 right, 15 left, 18 right, 21 right, 24
left, 25, 26, 31 left, 33 right, 36 right, 37, 39, 41, 44 right,
46–7; Getty Images p. 51 (Imagebank); Natural Visions
p. 48 (Heather Angel); Naturepl p. 30 (John Cancalosi);
NHPA pp. 5, 5 top, 6–7, 7, 8, 9 right, 10, 11 left, 12 left,
13, 15 right, 17, 19, 21 left, 20, 22–3, 23, 24 right, 26–7,
27, 28, 29 right, 33 left, 35 bottom, 38, 40, 43 right, 45
left, 45 right, 46 left, 48–9, 50–1; Oxford Scientific Films
pp. 9 left, 38; Photodisc pp. 4, 18 left; Premaphotos
Wildlife pp. 5 middle, 31 right, 34–5, 40–1 (Rod Preston-
Mafham); Science Photo Library pp. 5 bottom (Sinclair
Stammers), 6 (Susumu Nishinaga), 12 (Eye of Science), 14
(Sinclair Stammers), 22 (Sinclair Stammers), 29 left
(Claude Nuridsany & Marie Perennou), 36 left (Dr Jeremy
Burgess), 42 (Andrew Syred), 43 left (Dr P. Marazzi),
50 (Rosenfeld Images Ltd)

Cover photograph of a Plexippus jumping spider
reproduced with permission of FLPA (Minden
Pictures/Gerry Ellis)

The Publishers would like to thank Jon Pearce for his
assistance in the preparation of this book.

Disclaimer
All the Internet addresses (URLs) given in this book were
valid at the time of going to press. However, due to the
dynamic nature of the Internet, some addresses may have
changed, or sites may have changed or ceased to exist since
publication. While the author and Publishers regret any
inconvenience this may cause readers, no responsibility for
any such changes can be accepted by either the author or
the Publishers.

Contents

Any words appearing in the text in bold, **like this**, are explained in the Glossary. You can also look out for some of them in the 'Wild words' bank at the bottom of each page.

Amazing arachnids!

Can you believe it?
The largest arachnid is the emperor scorpion (below). It is found in the tropical forests and plains of Africa and can grow to 20 centimetres (8 inches) in length.

Arachnids are all around us and most are harmless. Spiders are probably the best known arachnids. Scorpions, ticks, mites, and harvestmen are also arachnids.

There are about 75,000 different kinds, or **species,** of arachnid in the world. None of them has a backbone. The easiest way to tell an arachnid from an insect is to count its legs. Arachnids all have eight legs. Insects have only six legs.

The smallest arachnids are mites. Many of them can only be seen with a **microscope.**

microscope an instrument that makes things look much bigger than they are

Did you know?

Arachnids do not have a skeleton like humans do. Instead they have a tough shell on the outside.

We need arachnids because they help to keep the balance in nature. They eat huge numbers of insects that harm plants, animals, and people.

Very few arachnids are harmful to humans, but many people are frightened of them. Fear of spiders is called **arachnophobia**.

Find out later...

... which arachnid has pincers like these.

... which arachnid has the deadliest bite.

... which arachnid can drink your blood.

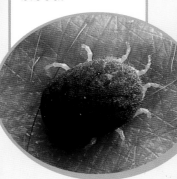

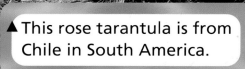
▲ This rose tarantula is from Chile in South America.

Meet the family

Spiders

Arachnids live on land in many different **habitats**. Some live in very cold places. Others live in baking hot deserts.

Spiders are found all over the world. If you climbed the highest mountain you would find spiders. There are over 40,000 different **species** of spider. Most of them live on land.

As well as eight legs, a spider usually has eight eyes. Its body is protected by a thin shell. As it gets bigger, it **sheds** its shell and grows a new one.

Walking on the ceiling!

Spiders can walk upside down because they have tiny claws with little hairs that stick to smooth surfaces. The claws also help the spider to cling to its web.

claws

Wild words   species type of living animal or plant

Fast food

Spiders have to be quick or clever to catch their **prey**. Lots of spiders make webs to trap their victims. Some spiders creep along the ground and grab passing insects.

Once they have caught their prey, most spiders stab it with their sharp **pincers**. The poison in the pincers kills or **paralyses** the prey.

Spiders are not insects

People often think spiders are insects. There are two important differences.

Spiders have eight legs. Insects have only six legs.

Most insects, such as butterflies, have wings and can fly. Spiders cannot fly, but they can jump!

▼ Hairs on the spider's legs can feel any movement nearby.

▲ Jumping spiders leap through the air to catch prey.

Scorpion fact file

Some scorpions are as small as a matchbox. Others are as big as the width of this page.

Most live for 3–5 years, but some can live 10–15 years. They have been known to live for 24 years.

Scorpions around the world

Scorpions live in every continent in the world apart from Antarctica, where it is very cold. Many of them live in deserts. Others live in forests and caves.

Night-time creatures

Scorpions mainly hunt at night. A scorpion can feel very small movements in the air or on the ground with tiny hairs that cover its body. This is how it senses that **prey** is coming.

▲ A cockroach makes a tasty snack for a scorpion.

Scorpion's sting

The scorpion has five **segments** in its tail, so it can bend it right up. The sting is in the last segment, at the end of the tail. It is shaped like an onion, and has **venom**, or poison, inside.

When a **predator** comes near, the scorpion bends up its tail. It is ready to defend itself. As the scorpion strikes, its sting injects venom into the predator.

Scorpions in Arizona

There are at least 30 **species** of scorpion in the state of Arizona in the USA.

Scorpions only sting if they feel frightened. This scorpion is ready to strike.

▲ Scorpions often **shed** their old skins in one piece.

predator animal that kills and eats other animals

A big family

Arachnids are part of an even bigger group, called **arthropods.** It includes many smaller animals that are not spiders or scorpions, but are very much like them. Here we meet a few of these animals.

Harvestmen

Harvestmen do not have **venom** like true spiders, but they have very long, thin legs and small bodies. They can run very fast. Harvestmen can catch and eat **venomous** spiders such as the deadly Australian redback spider.

Long legs

Harvestmen are sometimes called daddy-longlegs. This name is more often given to the crane fly.

▶ Harvestmen feed on ripe fruit and small animals.

arthropod animal with jointed legs but no backbone

Sun spiders

You might think sun spiders like the sun. They do not. Most of them come out at night. They live in hot dry areas including India, western USA, and Mexico.

Sun spiders are not true spiders. They only use three pairs of legs for running. Their front legs are more like **antennae**, or feelers. They also have bigger jaws than true spiders. They catch insects and tear them apart with their jaws.

▲ This sun spider lives in the Kalahari Desert in Africa.

Mini scorpions

Imagine a scorpion small enough to fit on the end of your pencil!

False scorpions are tiny relatives of true scorpions. They are often only 2–3mm (one tenth of an inch) long and are quite harmless. They do not have a sting. False scorpions catch tiny creatures with their claws.

antenna   (more than one are called antennae)   feeler on an insect's head   11

Mites

Mites and ticks also belong to the arachnid family. There could be between 25,000 and 50,000 **species** of mite around the world.

Many mites live on people and animals. They can cause disease. Some live on plants and stop them from growing properly. Most mites live in the soil and in rotting leaves. There could be millions in your garden or even in your house right now.

Holding tight

Adult ticks have mouth hooks. They use these to cling onto an animal so that they can feed on it. This one has burrowed through an animal's fur to get to its skin.

► This tiny red mite is feeding on a harvestman.

parasite animal or plant that lives in or on another living thing

Ticks

Some kinds of ticks are so tiny that you cannot see them. Others are as big as a drawing pin. They are **parasites**. This means they need to live on other animals including humans to get food.

A tick waits on leaves or tall grass until an animal passes. Then the tick jumps onto the animal and drinks its blood. When the tick's body is swollen with blood, it drops off.

Did you know?

Some people are **allergic** to the droppings of tiny dust mites. Their powdery poo floats in the air and makes it difficult for people who have **asthma** to breathe.

A dust mite is smaller than this full stop.

◄ Dust mites float in the air with dust. Here we can see them through a **microscope**. The dust mites are the things with hairs.

allergic having a bad reaction

Amazing bodies

Ancient scorpions

This **fossil** sea scorpion is 440 million years old. It has **gills** like a fish. This shows that it lived in water.

Sea scorpions grew to 2 metres (6 feet) long – the height of a tall man.

Blue-blooded spiders

Spiders do not have red blood like we do. Their blood is light blue. A spider's heart is not shaped like ours. It is more like a long tube. Their lungs are very different from ours too.

If you open a book and fan the pages out, you will get an idea of what a spider's lungs look like. They are actually called book lungs. Air gets into the lungs through narrow slits in the back part of the spider's body.

Breathing under water

Most spiders will quickly drown in water, but one species lives in water. The water spider makes its own silk air bubble under the water. It takes its **prey** back to the bubble and eats it.

When it needs more air, the water spider swims to the surface. There it collects air on its furry **abdomen** and then takes it back to the bubble.

fossil remains of something that lived very long ago, found in rock or mud

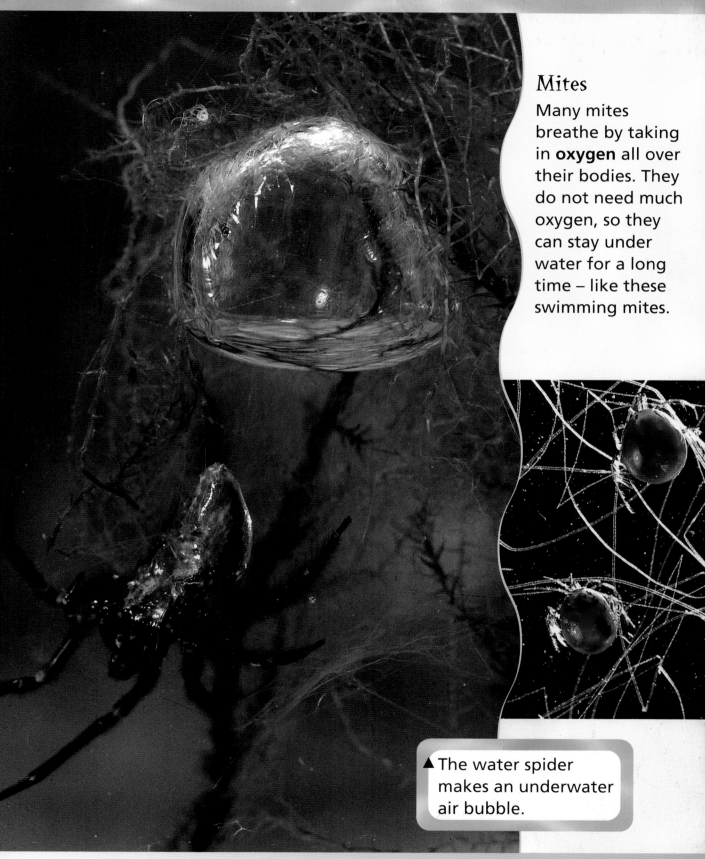

Mites

Many mites breathe by taking in **oxygen** all over their bodies. They do not need much oxygen, so they can stay under water for a long time – like these swimming mites.

▲ The water spider makes an underwater air bubble.

Hot and cold

Scorpions can survive the baking hot desert sun and the freezing cold desert nights.

Survival

Scorpions can go for as long as a year without food. They can eat a big meal all at once but they use up food very slowly, so it lasts a long time.

They do not need very much **oxygen** to **survive** either. The Andes Mountains in South America are over 4000 metres high. The air at the top of the mountains is very thin. People find it hard to breathe, but scorpions live there.

► Spiders live near the top of Mount Everest, the highest mountain in the world.

survive stay alive despite danger and difficulties

The highest creatures on Earth

In the 1920s a group was climbing on Mount Everest, in the Himalayas in Asia – the highest mountain in the world. They were surprised to find tiny, black, attid spiders living at 7000 metres above **sea level**. This is the highest **inhabited** place on Earth. The spiders live in cracks in the rocks and ice.

Dry as dust

Scorpions live in dry places, so they keep all their water inside their bodies. Their poo is just powdery dust.

sea level the place half way between high and low tide from which the height of all land is measured

Feeding

Spider webs

Spiders wait in their webs. They rush out when they feel a tug and kill or **paralyse** their prey.

There is enough silk in a spider web to stretch the length of a swimming pool.

Catching food

All spiders can make silk. It is very thin, but very strong. Some spiders spin a single thread. They can drop down on this to grab their **prey**.

Many spiders spin sticky webs to catch and hold insects. The spider can store its food in its web until it is hungry.

▼ Some spiders catch prey even bigger than themselves.

paralyse stun an animal so it is not able to move

Web design

Round webs like the one on the far left are not the only kind of web. House spiders make a **funnel** with a den at the end where they can hide and wait. The net-casting spider holds a net that it has made. It catches insects in the net.

Spiders may make new webs every day. Some spiders eat their old web. Others roll it into a ball and throw it away.

Can you believe it?

Spider silk is so strong that it has been used for fishing nets in Papua New Guinea.

◀ This spider is using its thread to slide down.

funnel cone shape

The biggest webs

Orb-webs can be up to 2 metres (6 feet) across. That is as tall as a man. They catch small birds and bats.

Finding food

Most scorpions sit at the entrance to their burrow. They wait for **prey** to walk past. Others go out hunting with their claws wide open. Their claws spring shut quickly on any prey that bumps into them.

One group of spiders are known as spitting spiders. They **paralyse** their prey by spitting a mixture of **venom** and glue onto them.

► This spitting spider has caught a mosquito.

orb-web circular web made by many spiders to catch insects

Good eyesight

The zebra spider has large front eyes that work rather like a zoom lens in a camera. They help it to spot prey that is a long way off.

The spider sits high up on a rock or wall, waiting for insects to come past. It can jump a long way to catch one.

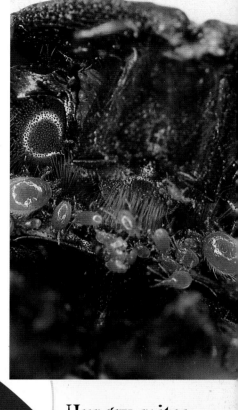

Hungry mites
The mites above are feeding on a beetle.

▲ A zebra spider will turn its head to look at you.

venom poison

Danger

There are hundreds of types of tick, but very few affect humans and pets. If you do find a tick on your skin, it is wise to see a doctor.

Ticks spread Lyme disease. Though it is very rare, this disease can kill people.

Blood suckers

Ticks feed on deer, sheep, cattle, dogs, cats, and humans. They need to hold on tight. A tick sinks its sharp **pincers** into the animal's skin and hooks itself on. As it sucks up blood, its body swells up like a pea. When it is full, it drops off. The tick digests its meal and then waits for another **host** animal to come along.

pincers hooks at the front of the mouth for holding prey

Life cycle

When a tick hatches from its egg it only has six legs. It is called a **larva**. It needs to suck blood from an animal to grow and change into a **nymph** with eight legs. After another feed it changes again and becomes an adult.

▼ After filling up with blood, the female tick lays her eggs.

Taking off a tick

Use tweezers to hold the tick firmly, as close to the skin as possible.

Pull slowly and carefully outward without twisting the tick. Clean the skin with disinfectant.

nymph young insect that looks like an adult in shape, but has no wings

Eating mum

Many female spiders die after laying their eggs. Their bodies are food for the newly-hatched babies.

Scorpions' soup

Scorpions have tiny mouths and can only eat liquid food. When they have killed their **prey**, they tear the flesh. Then they spit special **digestive juices** into the prey's insides. These juices turn it into soup that the scorpion can suck up.

▲ Black scorpions in the Sahara Desert quickly kill prey such as this gecko.

digestive juices acid and liquid made in the stomach to break down food

Spider's supper

Like scorpions, spiders only eat liquid or mushy food. The **venom** that a spider injects into its prey also contains digestive juices. These turn the insect's body into mush that the spider can eat. After its meal, the spider takes a nap while it digests the food.

Mite bites

Red spider mites eat plant juices. Some mites feed on animals.

Nearly every animal has mites living on it. The ones that live on you are mostly harmless.

◄ These red spider mites have been magnified. They are really only the size of a pinhead.

Breeding

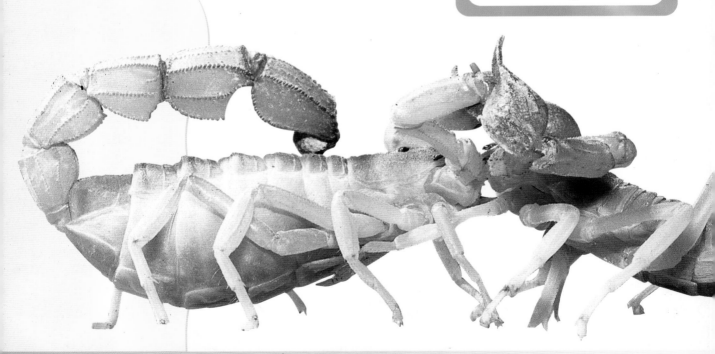

To make sure that their **species** will survive, arachnids, like all other types of animals, **breed** or reproduce.

For scorpions, breeding can be dangerous because scorpions tend to eat each other. Females are usually bigger, so the male may turn into dinner if he does not make a quick getaway.

Lifespan

Female tarantulas can live for up to 20 years. Males live only two or three years.

▼ The male scorpion, on the right, will need to escape quite quickly after mating.

breed to produce young

Dancing spiders

Female wolf spiders will only **mate** with a male who dances. She can tell by the dance if he is the right sort of spider to mate with. Females use chemicals like perfume to tell the males that they want to mate.

The female lays her eggs in a silky **cocoon** and then usually leaves them alone. The baby spiders must look after themselves when they hatch.

Parting

After mating, some female spiders kill the males, but most just leave the male alone.

▲ The male wolf spider is smaller than the female.

cocoon protective case made of silk

Water birth

Most water mites lay eggs wrapped in jelly. They stick them onto plant stems and floating leaves.

Birth

Most arachnids lay eggs, but scorpions do not. The females carry the **fertilized** eggs in their bodies. It can take a few months, or even a year, for the young to be born.

Some young scorpions look just like adults when they are born, except that their skin is soft and white. They are easy food for **predators** before they grow their hard shells.

▼ A water mite swims to a place to lay its eggs.

fertilize when a sperm joins an egg to form a new living thing

Nursery spiders

The female nursery web spider is likely to eat the male, so he gives her an insect to keep her busy. She eats this while they **mate**, and then the male tries to escape.

The female carries the eggs around until they are ready to hatch. Then she makes a little tent, called a nursery web, to protect the young.

Ballooning

Many newly-hatched spiders send out fine threads of silk. The breeze catches the threads and the spiders are whisked up into the air. This is called ballooning.

The lucky ones come down to Earth in places where they can find lots of food.

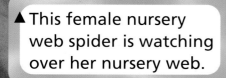
▲ This female nursery web spider is watching over her nursery web.

mate a male and female come together to produce young

Home with mum

A mother emperor scorpion lets her young live in her burrow. They may **hibernate** together.

Baby carriers

Some scorpion mothers hold their **pincers** as a 'birth basket' to catch the young as they are born. The young then climb onto their mother's back. She carries them around for about a week until they have **shed** their first skin. Sometimes they stay longer.

The young feed on the leftovers from their mother's meals. Male scorpions do not look after their young.

▶ A female emperor scorpion carries her young.

hibernate slow down the body so the animal appears to sleep for a long time

Cosy cocoons

All female spiders spin **cocoons**, silky cases to hold their eggs until they hatch. Some females leave as soon as they have laid eggs. Others stay and guard their cocoon.

The female wolf spider carries her cocoon around. The young spiders climb onto their mother's back as soon as they hatch. They stay there for about a week until they can **survive** on their own.

Caring mothers

Mothercare spiders are among the few who look after their young. The female below is feeding her babies by spitting food into their mouths.

▲ A mother wolf spider provides a taxi service for her young.

Defence

The **venom** that arachnids make helps to protect them from **predators**. Some animals will be put off by seeing a scorpion's tail raised ready to sting.

If an animal does attack, the scorpion will sting, and its venom may kill the attacker. Large scorpions also use their strong **pincers** to defend themselves.

Deadly

The yellow fat-tailed scorpion has probably killed more people than any other. The death **stalker** (right), that lives in North Africa and the Middle East, has even stronger venom.

stalk hunt by creeping up on a victim

Scorpions and people

People often think that scorpions are very dangerous, but only about 20 **species** have venom strong enough to hurt a human.

The desert scorpion lives in Arizona, California, and Utah in the USA. If it stings you, it hurts a lot and the wound swells up. You might even foam at the mouth. But you would only die if you were **allergic** to the venom.

▼ This scientist is collecting venom to make an **antidote** for people who have been stung.

Dead in seven minutes

In North Africa, they say that the yellow fat-tailed scorpion (below) can kill a person in seven hours, and it can kill a dog in just seven minutes.

antidote medicine given to make a poison safe

The top six

The world's most venomous spiders:

1 wandering spider

2 banana spider

3 funnel-web spider

4 black widow

5 recluse spider

6 sac spider

Deadly spiders

Spiders do not go looking for people to bite. They only bite to defend themselves. For example, if a spider hides in an empty shoe and then someone puts their foot in it, the spider may bite as a defence.

The world's deadliest spiders include the wandering spider from Brazil and the **funnel**-web spiders from Australia. Their bites have enough **venom** to kill a person.

▼ The wandering spider from Brazil is the world's deadliest spider.

Famous killers

Australia is famous for its deadly spiders, but fewer than 30 people are known to have died there from spider bites. The redback and funnel-web spiders are most **venomous**. About 200 people are treated for spider bites every year.

Although it has strong venom, the US black widow spider is more likely to run away than bite. The Australian funnel-web spiders are much less scared and will attack when they are threatened.

Tarantulas

They are hairy, but not scary. Some tarantulas eat birds, but they are not deadly enough to kill a human.

▲ The bite of the funnel-web spider can be treated with an **antidote**.

venomous poisonous

Hide and seek

The colour of many spiders is very similar to the plants on which they live. This is called **camouflage**. It helps spiders to hide from **predators**. They can also take their **prey** by surprise.

Disguising her nest

This long-jawed orb spider camouflages her **egg sac** so it looks like a bird dropping. This will stop other animals from finding her eggs and eating them.

Hiding places

Many insects visit flowers, so they are good places for spiders to lie in wait. Flower spiders often look like part of the flower on which they live. This crab spider is well hidden in a poppy.

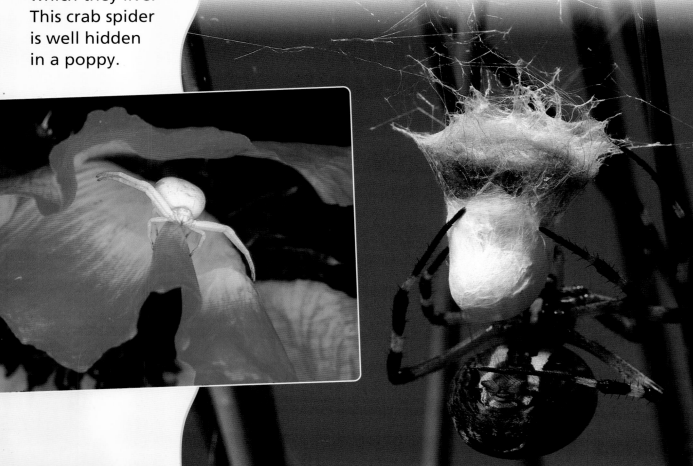

camouflage colours and patterns that match the background

Looks save lives

Orb-weaver spiders can hide from passing predators by stretching themselves out along the stem of a plant. They seem almost invisible.

Scorpions hide in their burrows in the daytime, so camouflage is not as important. Even so, scorpions that live in deserts are sandy-coloured. Rainforest scorpions are darker to blend with the shadows on the forest floor.

Bright mites

Predators know that bright colours usually mean that an animal is poisonous or tastes bad. Mites are often brightly coloured to stop predators from eating them.

Sand wolf spiders blend in well with the grains of sand.

egg sac small case that holds eggs

Escape

When it comes to escape, spiders are fast. They can throw out a silk thread and drop down from a tree, or run across to another branch quick as a flash!

The raft spider makes a fast getaway over a pond. It uses the tiny, **waterproof** hairs on its feet to trap pockets of air so that it can keep afloat.

Miraculous mites

Water mites have hairs all over their bodies. The hairs trap air bubbles so that the mites can breathe under water.

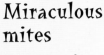

waterproof does not let in water

Keep off!

The tarantula has an interesting way of protecting itself. If a **predator** is about to attack, it shakes itself. This makes its hair fly off and get into the predator's eyes and mouth.

The whistling spider, an Australian tarantula, makes a loud, whistling noise when attacked. It is enough to make anyone jump, and frightens off predators.

Caught

Having a sting has not saved the scorpion in the picture below. Meerkats, like this one, rip off the sting before eating their **prey**. Some birds, centipedes, tarantulas, and lizards also enjoy a scorpion snack.

◄ A raft spider feels ripples on the water made by its prey.

Weird and wonderful

Spiders do some surprising things. Spitting spiders don't make webs. They just spit sticky silk to trap their **prey**.

Ant spiders pretend to be ants to avoid being eaten by birds and wasps. Not many **predators** eat ants, so the spiders are safe.

Tarantulas

Tarantulas only bite to defend themselves. Many of them live in burrows. Some South and Central American tarantulas live in trees. They are also found in Africa, Asia, and Australia.

Fear of spiders

Many people are frightened of spiders, especially the American black widow spider that can kill a human. Few people are harmed by them. A spider expert said, "the black widow may strike fear in people, but its bad name is unfair. In 33 years, I can't recall anyone dying from a black widow bite."

Superstition

In some countries it is considered unlucky to kill a spider. Next time you find one in the bath, do not wash it down the plughole. Spiders help to destroy pests.

◄ You can tell a black widow spider from the hourglass shape on it.

Itchy

- Bird mites live on the skin of many birds.

- Bee mites live in the breathing tubes of bees and can infect a whole hive.

Mini mites

Mites are too small to see and yet sometimes we can feel them. Many different kinds of mite live on or underneath the skin of animals and humans.

Tiny **follicle** mites get into human hair follicles and sweat glands. When they bite, it feels itchy and you want to scratch. They may be annoying, but they are not dangerous.

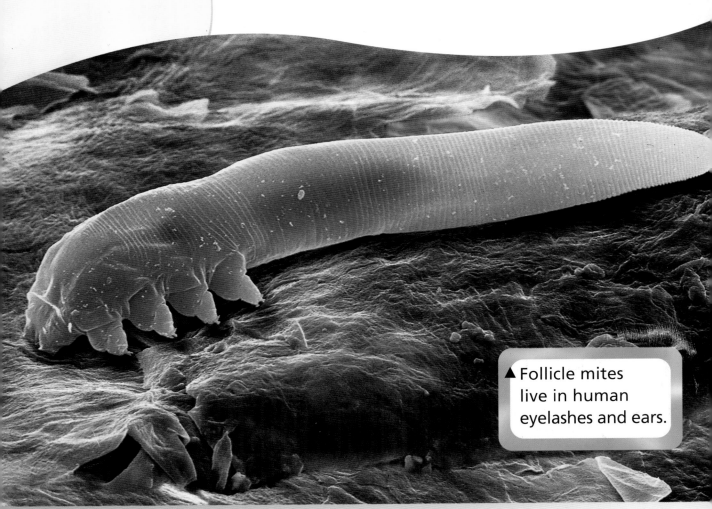

▲ Follicle mites live in human eyelashes and ears.

follicle small hole in the skin

Scabies and chiggers

Scabies mites tunnel into skin and lay their eggs. The **larvae** that hatch cause a lot of itching and often a rash of blisters, like the ones in the picture below.

Chiggers also pierce skin and cause itching. They are the larvae of bright red, harvest mites that are found on the soil in the USA. A chigger will inject **venom** into the bite, which makes it itchy.

Dry ticks

You are less likely to get ticks if you live near water. Scientists have discovered that ticks like dry places, and hide under leaves in winter. If they get wet when it is very cold, they may freeze to death.

◄ Scratching scabies makes the skin sore.

scabies skin disease caused by mites that makes the skin very itchy

Scorpion snacks

The black emperor scorpion may be the biggest, but it only weighs as much as a chicken's egg. It lives in the forests in Africa and eats insects, small birds and other small animals.

Although its **venom** isn't strong enough to kill a human, it keeps most **predators** away. But baboons are not scared of black emperors. They just rip off the sting before crunching up a tasty snack.

▶ This baboon is digging for scorpions in Africa.

Giant spiders

The largest tarantula is the Goliath bird-eating spider which lives in the tropical rainforests of South America. It could just reach its toes round the top and bottom of this book.

The Goliath bird-eating spider does not eat a lot of birds. It uses its long **pincers** to kill mostly insects, lizards, and frogs. It also eats mice. If there is not enough food, tarantulas can go for months without eating.

▲ Tarantulas have long, powerful pincers.

Tarantula facts

- Tarantulas can be as small as a fingernail or as large as a dinner plate.
- They have tiny claws that go in and out, like a cat's claws.
- They lose their hair when they get old.

▲ A Goliath bird-eating spider.

Arachnids in danger

Many animals find it hard to **survive** as humans cut down forests and destroy wild areas.

Arachnids are under threat from poisons used as **pesticides**, and from the **pollution** caused by chemicals and rubbish.

In British Columbia, in Canada, grassland has been ploughed up to grow grapes and other crops. This has meant that sun spiders do not have as much land as they need. They are at risk. Protecting wild areas may help to stop some arachnids from disappearing forever.

For sale in Peru

Spiders and butterflies are captured and killed in the rainforests to sell to collectors.

▲ Forest fires can destroy millions of arachnids in one day.

pesticide poison sprayed on crops to kill insects and pests

At risk

Some arachnids are **endangered** because they are caught and sold as pets. The Mexican red-kneed tarantula has bright, orange-red markings around the middle of each leg. It has been a popular pet for over 30 years. These spiders are now endangered. They can no longer be sold unless they have been bred in **captivity**.

Endangered tarantulas and scorpions have been found in the post in Australia. It is against the law to sell them, but smugglers hope to make a lot of money by selling them.

Last few left

There are very few cream-coloured tooth cave spiders left. They live in caves in Texas in the USA, but many of these have been filled in. These rare spiders need help.

endangered in danger of dying out

▶ A yellow-billed hornbill enjoys a scorpion meal.

Mites on the menu

Many animals make a meal of mites. Ants, beetles, harvestmen, other mites, small spiders, frogs, birds, and lizards all like to eat them.

immune protected by the body's defence system

Tasty scorpions

Humans are not the only threat to scorpions. Some **predators** like to eat scorpions so much, that they do not mind getting stung. Birds, bats, and lizards, as well as meerkats and baboons, are not put off. It is thought they may even become **immune** to the scorpion's **venom**. Grasshopper mice that regularly eat scorpions are not affected by the venom. They probably get immunity from their mothers.

Succulent spiders

Spiders have to watch out too. Birds, snakes, and scorpions all like to make a meal of them. Spider wasps hunt for spiders so they can inject their eggs into them. When the **larvae** hatch, they feed on the spider. They dig into its body, gradually killing it.

Endangered?

We do not know very much about mites. Some of the animals that mites live on are **endangered**. If these **host** animals die out, their mites may disappear as well.

---

host animal or plant that has a parasite living in or on it

Research
Scientists are using scorpion **venom** to develop drugs that will help with organ transplants and diseases. Instead of harming people, scorpion venom could cure them.

Arachnids and us

We do not know how many **species** of mite there are, but they are everywhere. Huge numbers live in the soil and in fresh water. Mites live on the smallest insects and the largest animals. Some mites and ticks spread disease to people, animals, and crops, but arachnids stop our planet from being overrun by insects. Arachnids, like all other creatures, have a job to do in keeping the balance in nature.

▶ Venom is taken from a **funnel**-web spider to use as an **antidote**. It will be given to someone when they have been bitten by a spider.

Protecting spiders

Spiders are everywhere. There could be over 50,000 spiders in an area the size of a football pitch. It is important to protect them because they help to keep the numbers of insects down.

When **pesticides** are used on crops, they kill spiders and helpful insects as well as the ones we call pests. We need to use other, natural ways of controlling pests, rather than spraying them with chemicals.

Sweet dreams

Scientists think that we probably eat about eight spiders in our lifetime. You may have eaten one or two already, without knowing it! It usually happens at night when a spider crawls across the pillow, but do not worry, it does not happen every night.

Find out more

Websites

BBC Nature
Information and quizzes about all aspects of nature.
www.bbc.co.uk /sn

Ecowatch
Photos and information about all sorts of incredible creatures.
www.ento.csiro. au/Ecowatch

Animal Discovery
Facts and fun about all kinds of animals.
www.animal. discovery.com

Books

Animals of the Rainforest: Tarantulas, Christy Steele (Raintree, 2003)

Killer Creatures: Spider, Tony Allan and David Jefferis (Belitha, 2002)

Minibeasts: Spiders, Claire Llewellyn (Franklin Watts, 2000)

Secret World of Spiders, Theresa Greenaway (Raintree, 2003)

World wide web

To find out more about arachnids you can search the Internet. Use keywords like these:

- arachnid
- spiders +scorpions
- "red spider mites"

You can find your own keywords by using words from this book. The search tips opposite will help you find useful websites.

Search tips

There are billions of pages on the Internet. It can be difficult to find exactly what you are looking for. These tips will help you find useful websites more quickly:

- Know what you want to find out about
- Use simple keywords
- Use two to six keywords in a search
- Only use names of people, places or things
- Put double quote marks around words that go together, for example "red spider mites"

Where to search

Search engine
A search engine looks through millions of website pages. It lists all the sites that match the words in the search box. You will find the best matches are at the top of the list, on the first page.

Search directory
A person instead of a computer has sorted a search directory. You can search by keyword or subject and browse through the different sites. It is like looking through books on a library shelf.

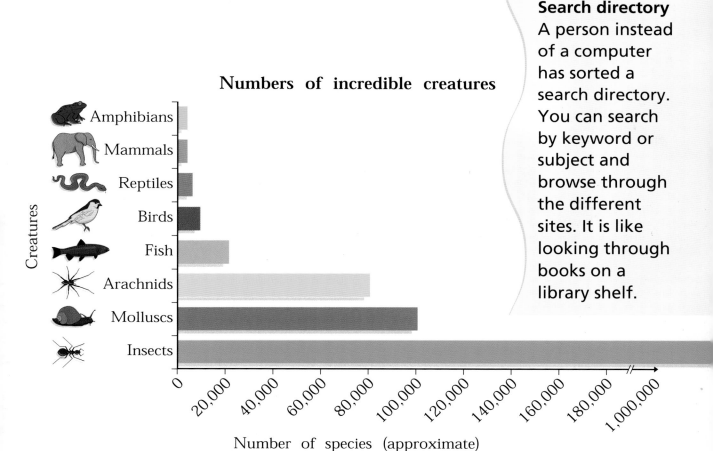

Numbers of incredible creatures

Creatures (vertical axis): Amphibians, Mammals, Reptiles, Birds, Fish, Arachnids, Molluscs, Insects

Number of species (approximate): 0, 20,000, 40,000, 60,000, 80,000, 100,000, 120,000, 140,000, 160,000, 180,000, 1,000,000

Glossary

abdomen rear part of the body, containing the stomach

allergic having a bad reaction

antenna (more than one are called antennae) feeler on an insect's head

antidote medicine given to make a poison safe

arachnophobia fear of spiders

arthropod animal with jointed legs but no backbone

asthma allergic reaction that affects the lungs and makes it hard to breathe

breed to produce young

camouflage colours and patterns that match the background

captivity enclosed space where humans keep animals

cocoon protective case made of silk

digestive juices acid and liquid made in the stomach to break down food

egg sac small case that holds eggs

endangered in danger of dying out

fertilize when a sperm joins an egg to form a new living thing

follicle small hole in the skin

fossil remains of something that lived very long ago, found in rock or mud

funnel cone shape

gills delicate, feathery structures that allow some animals to breathe under water

habitat natural home of an animal or plant

hibernate slow down the body so the animal appears to sleep for a long time

host animal or plant that has a parasite living in or on it

immune protected by the body's defence system

inhabited having animals living there

larva (more than one are called larvae) young form of an animal that looks very different from the adult

mate a male and female come together to produce young

microscope an instrument that makes things look much bigger than they are

nymph young insect that looks like an adult in shape, but has no wings

orb-web circular web made by many spiders to catch insects

oxygen one of the gases in air and water that all living things need

paralyse stun an animal so it is not able to move

parasite animal or plant that lives in or on another living thing

pesticide poison sprayed on crops to kill insects and pests

pincers hooks at the front of the mouth for holding prey

pollution damage caused by chemicals, fumes, and rubbish

predator animal that kills and eats other animals

prey animal that is killed and eaten by other animals

scabies skin disease caused by mites that makes the skin very itchy

sea level the place half way between high and low tide from which the height of all land is measured

segment section

shed get rid of, or lose

species type of living animal or plant

sperm sex cell produced by the male

stalk hunt by creeping up on a victim

survive stay alive despite danger and difficulties

waterproof does not let in water

venom poison

venomous poisonous

Index

Titles in the *Freestyle Express*: *Incredible Creatures* series include:

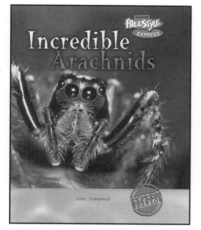

Hardback: 1844 434516

Hardback: 1844 434524

Hardback: 1844 434532

Hardback: 1844 434540

Hardback: 1844 434761

Hardback: 1844 43477X

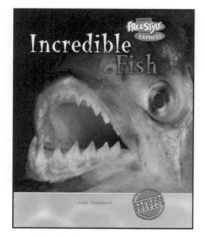

Hardback: 1844 435172

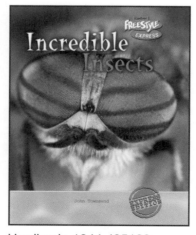

Hardback: 1844 435180

Find out about other Freestyle Express titles on our website www.raintreepublishers.co.uk